S0-ADD-889

PUPS IN THE PICTURES

AMANDA BERGLUND

GEORGE

BRINGING UP BABY
(1938)

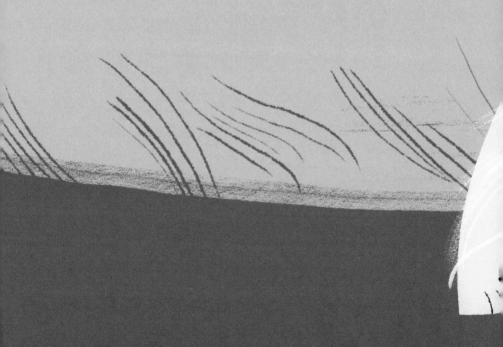

TOTO

THE WIZARD OF OZ
(1939)

LASSIE

LASSIE COME HOME
(1943)

FRED

SMOKEY AND THE BANDIT
(1977)

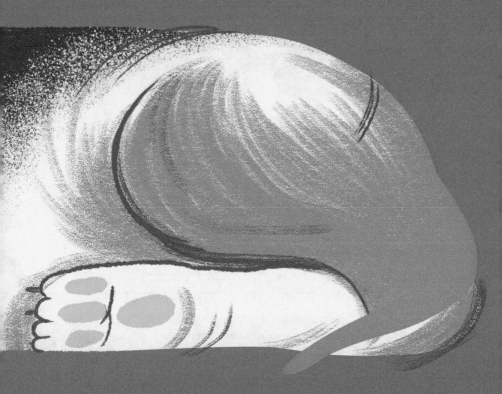

SHITHEAD

THE JERK
(1979)

DOG

**MAD MAX 2
(1981)**

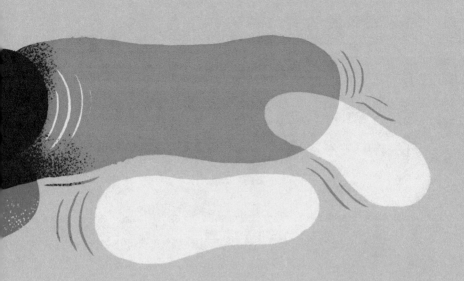

NANOOK

THE LOST BOYS
(1987)

SAM

LETHAL WEAPON
(1987)

HOOCH

**TURNER & HOOCH
(1989)**

QUARK

**HONEY I SHRUNK THE KIDS
(1989)**

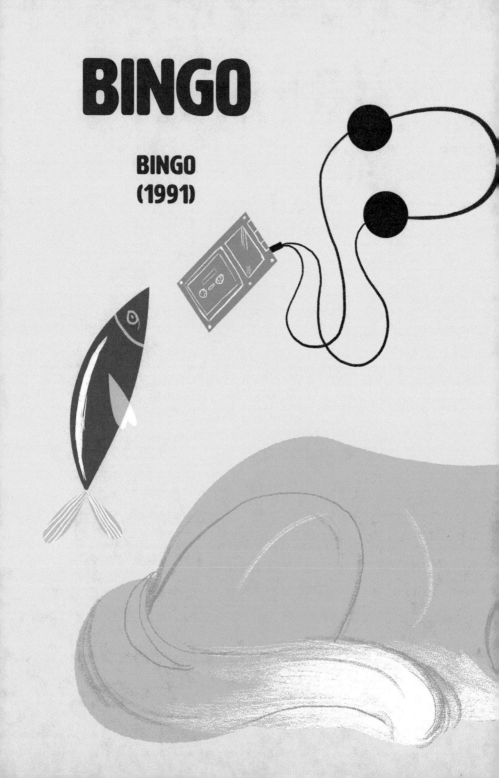

BINGO

BINGO
(1991)

BEETHOVEN

BEETHOVEN
(1992)

THE BEAST

THE SANDLOT
(1993)

FRANK

**MEN IN BLACK
(1997)**

BUDDY

AIR BUD
(1997)

BEATRICE

BEST IN SHOW
(2000)

WINKY

BEST IN SHOW
(2000)

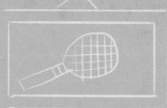

BUCKLEY

THE ROYAL TENENBAUMS
(2001)

BAXTER

ANCHORMAN
(2004)

SAMANTHA

I AM LEGEND
(2007)

JACK

THE ARTIST
(2011)

© AMANDA BERGLUND
AMANDABERGLUND.COM
2017